Henry Ford

HENRY FORD
(1863–1947)

QUOTATIONS
OF
Henry Ford

APPLEWOOD BOOKS
Bedford, Massachusetts

ISBN 978-1-55709-948-8

10 9 8 7 6 5 4 3

Printed in the U.S.A.

Henry Ford

HENRY FORD was born July 30, 1863, and grew up on his family's farm in what is today Dearborn, Michigan (about 10 miles from Detroit). From an early age Henry loved to tinker with all sorts of mechanical devices, and soon he developed a strong dislike for the drudgery of farm work.

In 1879 Henry left home for Detroit to become an apprentice machinist, and by 1891 was working for the Edison Illuminating Company, a steam-powered plant that generated electricity for over 100 customers. Henry was promoted to chief engineer in 1893 but had become so fascinated with internal combustion engines that he spent nearly all of his spare time building a gasoline-powered car in a shed behind the house he was renting. Henry called his car the Quadricycle and drove it for the first time in June 1896. Three years later, Henry gave up a promising career in the electric industry and set out to design and build automobiles.

Henry's first two automobile companies failed, but in 1903 the Ford Motor Company was incorporated and began assembling Ford's first production automobile, the Model A. With the introduction of the Model T in 1908 Henry finally realized his dream of producing an automobile "for the masses" that was rugged, dependable, and reasonably priced. This vehicle initiated a new era in personal transportation. It was easy to operate, maintain, and handle on rough roads, and quickly became a huge success. To meet the growing demand, Henry opened a large factory at Highland Park, Michigan, where precision manufacturing and a division of labor, as well as standardized and interchangeable parts, were combined with the moving assembly line. A new manufacturing process was created that revolutionized the automobile industry and made Ford Motor Company the largest automobile manufacturer in the world.

In addition to building automobiles, Henry helped pioneer commercial aviation; developed soy-based foods and plastics; and, in 1929, established the Edison Institute of Technology (now known as The Henry Ford), an indoor/outdoor museum complex dedicated to preserving over 300 years of American history. In 1947, Henry died at age 83 at Fair Lane, his Dearborn home.

Henry Ford's success made him a folk hero the world over, and he was frequently asked to give his opinions on a variety of subjects. Henry had only a grade school education and was uncomfortable speaking in public, so many of the sayings attributed to him over the years have been drawn from quips he made during actual interviews, from articles prepared for him by ghostwriters, and other sources. Taken as a whole, these quotations, whether uttered word for word by Henry Ford or not, are now part of a powerful "Ford myth" that speaks to his enormous impact on American society.

QUOTATIONS
OF
Henry
Ford

One of the greatest obstacles to a man's advancement is discontent.

Henry Ford

Because a thing is useful is no reason why it should be ugly.

Henry Ford

Business grows big through the service it renders, not through any 'control' that it exercises over materials, money or people.

Henry Ford

The conflict between the generations is as old as the natural consequence of human progress. Those who are coming on behind us are not our children in the sense that we have created them and defined their limitations; they are rather a new race, different from us in their equipment and outlook—quite likely to be much better than we are.

When business becomes so big that its bigness is a tax upon the community, instead of a service to the community, the decreasing patronage of the people becomes an effective check.

Henry Ford

Competition whose motive is merely to compete, to drive some other fellow out, never carries very far. The competitor to be feared is one who never bothers about you at all but goes on making his own business better all the time. Businesses that grow by development and improvement do not die.

Henry Ford

Profits made out of the distress of the people are always much smaller than profits made out of the most lavish service of the people at the lowest prices that competent management can make possible.

There is safety in small beginnings and there is unlimited capital in the experience gained by growing.

Henry Ford

The business itself does not fail; but the man who is "boss" of a business that he does not know to its last operative detail is certain of failure before he begins.

Henry Ford

The best road to the white collar is through blue-jeans and practical brains.

Henry Ford

It is a strange law that the larger the accomplishment, the less the work.

*B*usiness and Government both being necessary to the public welfare, why do evil results occur when they come together? An uneasy feeling oppresses the people when they see the two in agreement; they suspect that private interest in commerce is linked with the servants of private interest in politics.

Henry Ford

*B*etter one hundred little fellows all pushing ahead to make things go than one big fellow waiting for things to start.

Henry Ford

*O*ur conservative nature digests and makes our own what our radical nature has conquered. But neither conservatism nor radicalism is supreme, one never vanquishes the other, both are hands used by Life. Life uses radicalism now for a little; and now it uses conservatism for a little. Between them they measure the course of the weaver's shuttle, the great weaver, Destiny.

The return to conservatism means that the people have satisfied themselves that they are on the right track. They believe that they will reach the desired social and economic goal by progressing along the tested and proved path rather than by turning again into the wilderness.

Henry Ford

It has always been our belief that a sale does not complete the transaction between us and the buyer, but establishes a new obligation on us to see that the car gives good service. We are as much interested in your economical operation of the car as you are in our manufacture of it. For that reason we have installed a system of controlled service to take care of all Ford car needs in an economical and improved manner.

Our nation is composed of thousands of small communities. If a majority of these become centers of creative, gainful effort . . . , we need not worry about the future. Hand in hand with its increased material prosperity will develop social advantages and moral assets, which are the foundation of our American way of life.

Henry Ford

We are living in a great time. We are a bridge generation. What we found when we came upon the scene and what we shall leave to those who follow mark the transition from the old to the new. We have been the bridge. Complaints we hear about the seeming slowness of progress are mostly from those who would rather be the crossing throng than the bridge that carries them.

The industrial value of leisure as a promoter of the consumption of goods, and thus as a stimulant to business have been proved. People who have more leisure must have more clothes. They must have a greater variety of food, more transportation, more service of various other kinds. If we should come to a five-day week the result would be beneficial to industry and commerce. Instead of business being slowed up because the people were "off work," it would be speeded up because they would consume more in their leisure than in their working time.

Henry Ford

The only prosperity the people can afford to be satisfied with is the kind that lasts.

$\mathcal{T}$he wisdom of life is to keep on planting. Some . . . never plant after youthful imagination dies, and they reap only the one crop which they planted in youth. Plant every season and life will be a succession of harvests.

Henry Ford

$\mathcal{L}$ife is a going concern. It is going somewhere. It never stagnates. That is one reason I like to watch and talk with the youngsters at the schools in Greenfield Village. What I greatly hope for these children everywhere, is a new attitude toward life—free from the gullibility which thinks we can get something for nothing; free from the greed which thinks any permanent good can come of overreaching others; and, above all, expectant of change, so that when life gives them a jolt they will be fully prepared to push on eagerly along new lines.

The secrets of life are open to the thinker....
We prefer the swarm of other people's ideas
to our own thinking, because thinking is the
hardest kind of work a mortal can do. And just
because it is hardest, the higher rewards are
reserved to it. Thinking calls for facts; facts are
found by digging; but he who has gathered this
wealth is well equipped for life.

Henry Ford

An educated person enjoys life and is able
to create his own recreations; he can change
swiftly from one line of effort to another if
conditions require a change; he has poise, and
some kind of religion that he deeply respects.

Henry Ford

To resent efficiency is a mark of inefficiency.

Speech is one of man's most marvelous tools, and is a direct relation between the kind of speech which he uses and the kind of work which he does. A good and experienced engineer can tell what language a machine has been built in, just by looking at it.

Henry Ford

English language is the world's tool in industry, colonization, and the bringing of prosperity to every kind and degree of men. It is the World Language. The world accepts it because justice, freedom, prosperity and opportunity have higher meanings in English than in any other tongue.

Henry Ford

Any customer can have a car painted any color that he wants so long as it is black.

Henry Ford

Whether you think you can or whether you think you can't, you're right.

$\mathcal{A}$s betting at the race ring adds neither strength nor speed to the horse, so the exchange of shares in the stock market adds no capital to business, no increase in the production and no purchasing power to the market.

Henry Ford

$\mathcal{O}$ur pace is set by human beings like ourselves. Those who keep step feel the pace to be natural. Progress is geared to every man's gait. Being dragged along is where the strain comes in. Keeping step is keeping fit.

Henry Ford

$\mathcal{T}$he gifted man bears his gifts into the world, not for his own benefit, but for the people among whom he is placed; for the gifts are not his, he himself is a gift to the community. This is the way Life gives gifts to the people, it wraps them up in men, and sends them forth.

Good doctors help people whatever may be the system of medicine they use; and a good administration is a help no matter how crude the form of government may be.

Henry Ford

There is no failure except failure to serve one's purpose.

Henry Ford

The consent of the governed is always based on the service of the governed.

Henry Ford

If sometimes we seem to live in a time of little men, it may be only because there are so many big men that greatness does not seem unusual.

One purpose . . . of Greenfield Village and the Edison Institute and Museum [now The Henry Ford] is to remind the public who visit it . . . of how far and how fast we have come in technical progress in the last century or so. If we have come so far and so fast, is it likely that we shall stop now?

Henry Ford

The world is held together by the mass of honest folk who do their daily tasks, tend their own spot in the world, and have faith that at last the Right will come fully into its own. These are the salt of the earth, they constitute that saline solution which is forever reviving a moribund world. They believe that right motives make right conditions, that if their faces are turned toward the light they cannot miss the road, and all right-minded men desire to see this true faith of the people vindicated. This is our truest basis of prosperity. It is the essence of all our security. It is the promise of all our progress. If this faith should be lost from any considerable group of society, it would constitute a loss equal to that of all the material wealth we possess.

*T*o be good is not enough; a man must be good for something.

Henry Ford

*D*anger to our country is to be apprehended not so much from the influence of new things as from our forgetting the value of old things.

Henry Ford

I foresee the time when industry shall no longer denude the forests which require generations to mature, nor use up the mines which were ages in making, but shall draw its raw material largely from the annual produce of the fields. I am convinced that we shall be able to get out of yearly crops most of the basic materials which we now get from forest and mine.

I'm going to start up a museum and give people a true picture of the development of the country. That's the only history that is worth observing, that you can preserve in itself. We're going to build a museum that's going to show industrial history, and it won't be bunk! We'll show the people what actually existed in years gone by and we'll show them the actual development of American industry from the earliest days that we can recollect up to the present day.

Henry Ford

*T*he hand, no matter how dexterous, would be a useless piece of machinery were it not guided by intellect.

Henry Ford

*E*ducation is not preparation for life, but a part of life—a continuous part.

Henry Ford

*Y*ou can't build a reputation on what you're going to do.

Challenge the creators of fear and suspicion. Make them produce their facts, and line up facts alongside daily life as you know it.

Henry Ford

There is a high road and a low road to wisdom. All that we call science and wisdom is all about us. As the air was filled with voices unheard of by us until we put up aerials and made receivers, so is all we need to live and to know in the universe; it is ours to make the contact.

Henry Ford

No one loses anything by raising wages as soon as he is able. It has always paid us. Low wages are the most costly any employer can pay.

Just as the eight-hour day opened our way to prosperity in America, so the five-day week will open our way to still greater prosperity.

Henry Ford

Wages, regarded as an armistice between capital and labor, can yield no basic principle. But when regarded as one of the principal products of a business—as the dividends of production—there is hope of finding what they ought be.

Henry Ford

While we take great pleasure in giving employment to maimed men, we believe that we are doing a far greater work by preventing this maiming of men.

Henry Ford

When figures and philosophy agree, we are hitting near the truth.

*T*he so-called 'materialism' of the age is caused mostly by the lack of materials not by a deluge of them.

Henry Ford

*I*ndividualism is what makes cooperation worth living.

Henry Ford

I will build a motor car for the great multitude . . . . constructed of the best materials, by the best men to be hired, after the simplest designs that modern engineering can devise. . . so low in price that no man making a good salary will be unable to own one—and enjoy with his family the blessing of hours of pleasure in God's great open spaces.

The Model T Ford car was a pioneer. There was no conscious public need of motor cars when we first conceived it. The Ford car blazed the way for the motor industry and started the movement for good roads. It broke down the barriers of time and distance and helped to place education within the reach of all. It gave people more leisure. It helped people everywhere to do more and better work in less time and enjoy doing it. It did a great deal, I am sure, to promote the growth and progress of this country.

Henry Ford

Competition cannot be abolished; every attempted monopoly is an added impetus to a whole round of competitors. Big business, so far from destroying competition, only raises up bigger competitors.

The best way is always the simplest.

Henry Ford

There is on this continent almost every variety of scene that the wide world can furnish. There are mountains which for majesty and grandeur cannot be equaled in any other country; stately rivers, magnificent lakes, boundless woods, mighty waterfalls. In spite of improved highways and cheaper transportation, this vast heritage is not appreciated as it ought to be. We are always seeking for those things which are in the clouds, not for those that lie at our feet. It is not that which we hold in our hands or store away that makes up wealth, it is the faculty of fully appreciating and enjoying those things without which the world would be a vast sterile tract as devoid of beauty as the moon with its oceans of ashes and burnt-out craters, which nothing can redeem.

We are entering an era when we shall create resources which shall be so constantly renewed that the only loss will be not to use them. There will be such a plenteous supply of heat, light and power, that it will be a sin not to use all we want. This era is coming now. And it is coming by way of Water.

Henry Ford

The most closely organized groups and movements in the world are those which have been the least friendly to the people's progress and liberty.

Henry Ford

Success does not come by imitation.

$\mathcal{B}$e ready to revise any system, scrap any method, abandon any theory, if the success of the job requires it.

Henry Ford

$\mathcal{T}$here is no progress in merely finding a better way to do a useless thing.

Henry Ford

$\mathcal{T}$here comes a time, when instead of making dead branches less ugly, the ax should be laid at the root of the tree.

$\mathcal{P}$eople who say everything is going to pieces simply because the junk pile is growing, are looking only at one corner of the field.

Henry Ford

$\mathcal{D}$estructive radicalism is the foe of progress because it knows (and says) that betterment of social conditions neutralizes revolutionary activity. Hard-shell conservatism is the foe of progress because it thinks of human wealth in terms of the present quantity and is moved by unintelligent selfishness.

Henry Ford

$\mathcal{O}$ur modern industrialism, changed to motives of public service, will provide means to remove every injustice that gives soil for prejudice.

*T*he genius of the American people is Self-Reliance.

Henry Ford

*T*he great thing as I see it today is the back-to-the-land movement. This is the answer to the problem of how to make people self-sustaining rather than dependent upon industry which, at its best, is uncertain and seasonal. Whenever people learn to become self-sustaining on farms or in small rural communities, then industry will seek out these communities. Industry will follow people to smaller towns and many of our problems will be solved. For, when people become self-sustaining, they will soon start to accumulate a surplus. This surplus, in turn, will create new markets.

Henry Ford

*A*ny man can get what any man has got by making it.

One man's rule is another man's ruin.

Henry Ford

We begin as pensioners. Some people live two-thirds of their life on the provision made for them by others. We graduate into cooperators, earn our own living, hold up our own end of the job, produce a little extra for the pensioners that are coming on behind us. A few enter the third stage, where they do something more for the world than the world does for them. They put the world in their debt by making every man's living better, or his hope larger, or his opportunity wider. Just to hold up one's end of the load is a great and satisfactory thing; it makes one a man. However, it only squares the account. But to do for the world more than the world does for you—that is Success.

Henry Ford

It is easier to think wrongly than to feel wrongly.

History is more or less bunk. It is tradition. We don't want tradition. We want to live in the present, and the only history that is worth a tinker's damn is the history we make today.

Henry Ford

We are here for experience, and experience is a preparation to know the Truth when we meet it.

Henry Ford

The only true test of values, either of men or of things, is that of their ability to make the world a better place in which to live.

Henry Ford